Close-up Continents

✦ Mapping North America ✦

Paul Rockett

✦

with artwork by Mark Ruffle

W

FRANKLIN WATTS

LONDON • SYDNEY

Franklin Watts
This edition published in Great Britain in 2022
by Hodder & Stoughton

Copyright © Hodder & Stoughton, 2022

Editor: Adrian Cole
Series design and illustration: Mark Ruffle
www.rufflebrothers.com

Picture credits:
Aerial Archives.com/Alamy: 21t; All
Canada Photos/Alamy: 15t; NASA, courtesy
of Jacques Descloitres, MODIS Land Rapid
Response Team at NASA GSFC: 13b;
Photogenes: 8b; Wikimedia Commons: 6-7,
21b; Wollertz/Shutterstock: 17; Sergey
Yechikov/Shutterstock: 29; Zuma Press/Alamy:
25.

Every attempt has been made to clear
copyright. Should there be any inadvertent
omission please apply to the publisher for
rectification.

Dewey number: 917
ISBN: 978 1 4451 4104 6

Printed in Dubai

Franklin Watts
An imprint of Hachette Children's Group
Part of Hodder & Stoughton
Carmelite House
50 Victoria Embankment
London EC4Y 0DZ

An Hachette UK Company.
www.hachettechildrens.co.uk

MIX
Paper from
responsible sources
FSC® C104740
FSC
www.fsc.org

Contents

Where is North America?

North America is the third largest continent in the world and covers about 4.8 per cent of the Earth's surface. It's a continent filled with a wide range of wildlife, culture and climates, stretching down from the Arctic chill of Greenland to the tropical heat of Costa Rica's Cocos Island.

North America

North American regions

North America is made up of countries that are sometimes split into smaller regions.

USA and Canada

Some geographers consider North America to be just the USA and Canada.

Canada

USA

The Caribbean

The Caribbean refers to the Caribbean Sea and its chain of islands. Although part of North America, it is not attached to the mainland of the continent and so has a separate geographic identity.

Central America

The countries below the USA and above South America are sometimes grouped together as one region called Central America. This is because the shape of the land appears separate from the rest of North America, and the countries here share a similar culture and language.

South America

Latin America

The countries of Central America, the Caribbean and the continent of South America are sometimes grouped under the name Latin America. They were once part of empires ruled from southern Europe (see pages 8–9). As a result, most people here speak the Latin-based languages of Spanish or Portuguese.

Supercontinent

North America was once part of a supercontinent called Laurasia. It broke apart into separate continents some 66 million to 30 million years ago.

The Earth's surface is made up of tectonic plates that move slowly around, causing the break-up and creation of continents. North America sits on two tectonic plates, the North American Plate and the Caribbean Plate.

North
America

Europe and
Asia

South
America

Africa

Laurasia

Antarctica

North
American
Plate

Caribbean
Plate

Bering Land Bridge

Around 20,000 years ago Siberia (in Asia) and Alaska (in North America) were connected by a stretch of land called the Bering Land Bridge. This land is now under water. The first human inhabitants of North America are believed to have walked over the Bering Land Bridge from Asia.

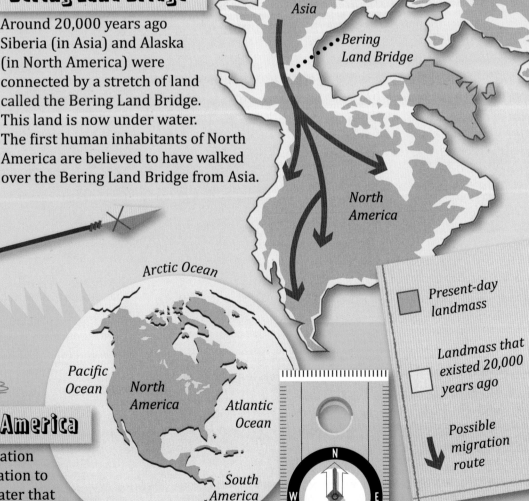

Asia

Bering
Land Bridge

North
America

Arctic Ocean

Pacific
Ocean

North
America

Atlantic
Ocean

South
America

Present-day
landmass

Landmass that
existed 20,000
years ago

Possible
migration
route

Locating North America

We can describe the location of North America in relation to the areas of land and water that surround it, as well as using the points on a compass.

- North America is west of the Atlantic Ocean
- The Arctic Ocean is north of North America
- North America is north of South America
- North America is east of the Pacific Ocean

Countries

North America is made up of 23 countries, but also includes a number of islands that are still under the rule of European countries. Its population has a diverse mix of backgrounds, descending from its indigenous peoples, colonial settlers, African slaves and immigrants from Europe and Asia.

Kingdom of Denmark

While Greenland is geographically part of North America, it is politically connected to Europe. It used to be a Danish colony and is still part of the Kingdom of Denmark.

Greenland
Greenland is the largest island in the world.

Canada

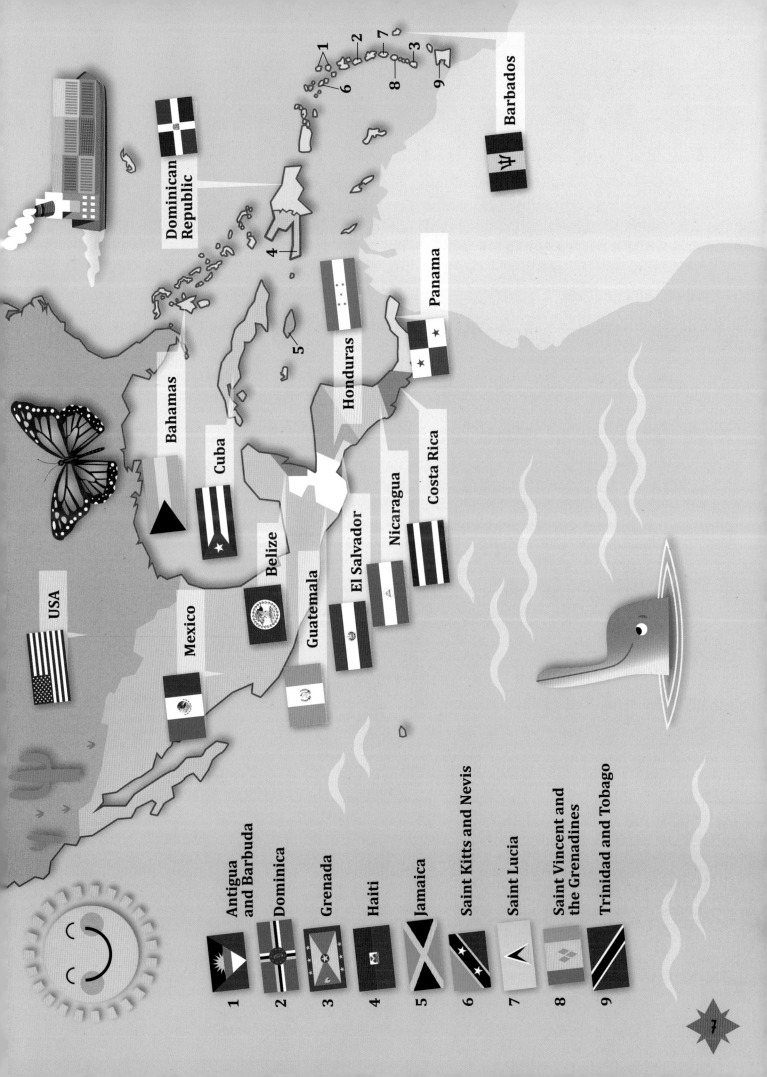

USA

Mexico

Bahamas

Cuba

Belize

Guatemala

El Salvador

Nicaragua

Honduras

Costa Rica

Panama

Dominican Republic

Barbados

1 Antigua and Barbuda
2 Dominica
3 Grenada
4 Haiti
5 Jamaica
6 Saint Kitts and Nevis
7 Saint Lucia
8 Saint Vincent and the Grenadines
9 Trinidad and Tobago

Columbus and before

The maps of North America that we use today were developed from those made by European explorers during the 15th and 16th centuries. Other types of map, made by the indigenous peoples of North America, recorded journeys for the land and sea.

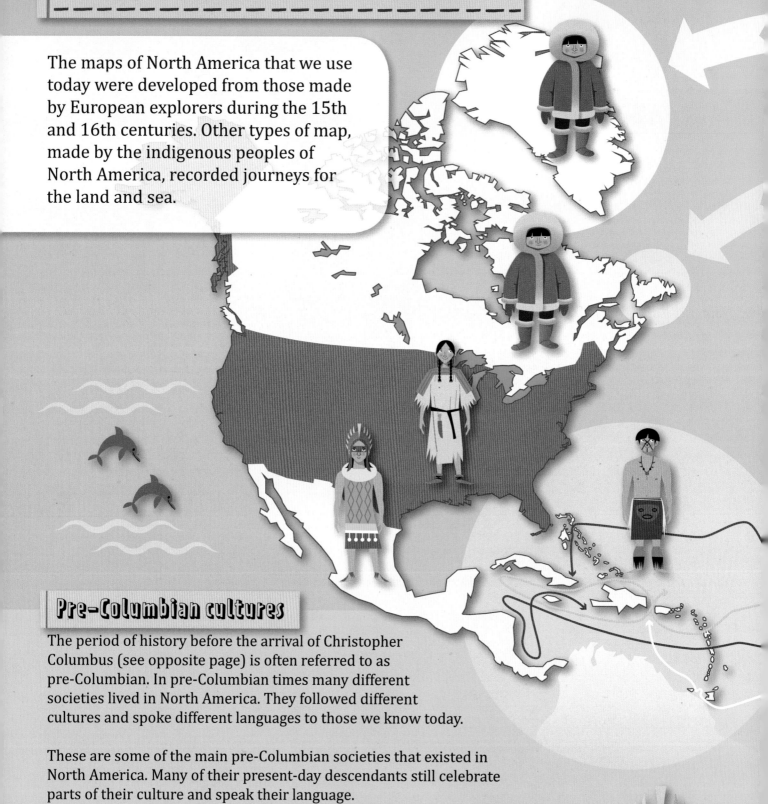

Pre-Columbian cultures

The period of history before the arrival of Christopher Columbus (see opposite page) is often referred to as pre-Columbian. In pre-Columbian times many different societies lived in North America. They followed different cultures and spoke different languages to those we know today.

These are some of the main pre-Columbian societies that existed in North America. Many of their present-day descendants still celebrate parts of their culture and speak their language.

Inuit

Native Americans

Arawak

Aztecs and Mayans

Inuit wooden maps

As long as 300 years ago, the Inuit, who live along the coast of Greenland, used wooden maps. These three-dimensional maps show the rugged coastline. They were carved from of a piece of wood, with bumps and notches representing fjords, islands and glaciers.

First European settlements

It's thought that the first Europeans to arrive in North America were the Vikings. They sailed to Greenland in the late 10th century and to Canada in the 11th century.

Christopher Columbus

In 1492, Christopher Columbus, an Italian explorer funded by Spain, set sail from Europe to find a route west to the continent of Asia. However, he didn't make it to Asia, and instead landed in the Bahamas.

Between 1492 and 1504 Columbus made four separate voyages to North America, exploring the Caribbean islands and the coast of Central America – areas previously unknown to Europe.

First voyage, 1492–1493

Second voyage, 1493–1496

Fourth voyage, 1502–1504

Third voyage, 1498–1500

The use of wood meant that the maps survived harsh weather conditions, and the carved shapes allowed the user to understand the geography of the area by feeling the map as much as looking at it.

Aztec codices

The Aztecs were a tribe that, from around 1345 to 1521, built up a powerful empire in northern Mexico. However their civilisation was wiped out by Spanish invaders (see page 20) and an outbreak of smallpox.

The Aztecs made codices – painted manuscripts made of one long sheet of paper folded up like an accordion. These featured pictures and symbols that recorded important events, family information and geographical landmarks.

This image is copied from the Aztec Codex Zouche-Nuttall. *The symbols of waterfalls and caves helped historians to find the actual location shown.*

Independent states

After the voyages of Columbus, large areas of North America were taken over by the European countries of Spain, France and Great Britain. These colonial powers, and independent rule for the colonies later on, all shaped the borders we recognise today.

European territory in North America, 1713

☐ = land claimed by Great Britain ■ = land claimed by Spain

☐ = land claimed by France ☐ = unorganised territory

Independence

Movements towards independence from European powers began in the 18th century. This changed the shape of many of North America's countries, with borders being redrawn across the continent.

USA

On 4 July 1776, thirteen British colonies declared independence and the United States of America was formed. It took the next 183 years for the remaining states to join the Union, making up the country that we recognise today.

Washington, Montana, North Dakota, Minnesota, Wisconsin, Michigan, New Hampshire, Vermont, Massachusetts, Connecticut, Maine, Oregon, Idaho, South Dakota, New York, Wyoming, Nevada, Utah, Nebraska, Iowa, Illinois, Indiana, Ohio, Pennsylvania, Rhode Island, New Jersey, Delaware, Maryland, California, Colorado, Kansas, Missouri, Kentucky, West Virginia, Virginia, Arizona, Oklahoma, Tennessee, North Carolina, New Mexico, Arkansas, Mississippi, Alabama, South Carolina, Georgia, Texas, Louisiana, Florida

The USA is made up of 50 states. Alaska is the 49th state and is in the northwest of North America, bordering Canada. The 50th state, Hawaii, is in the region of Australasia.

Alaska

Hawaii

The Stars and Stripes

The flag of the USA is often referred to as the 'Stars and Stripes'. The 50 stars represent the 50 states that make up the country. The 13 stripes represent the first 13 states that declared independence from colonial rule.

Canada

In 1763 France handed over its Canadian territories to Great Britain, and on 1 July 1867 the remaining British colonies in the north joined together to form the Dominion of Canada. Canadian Independence Day is celebrated each year on 1 July.

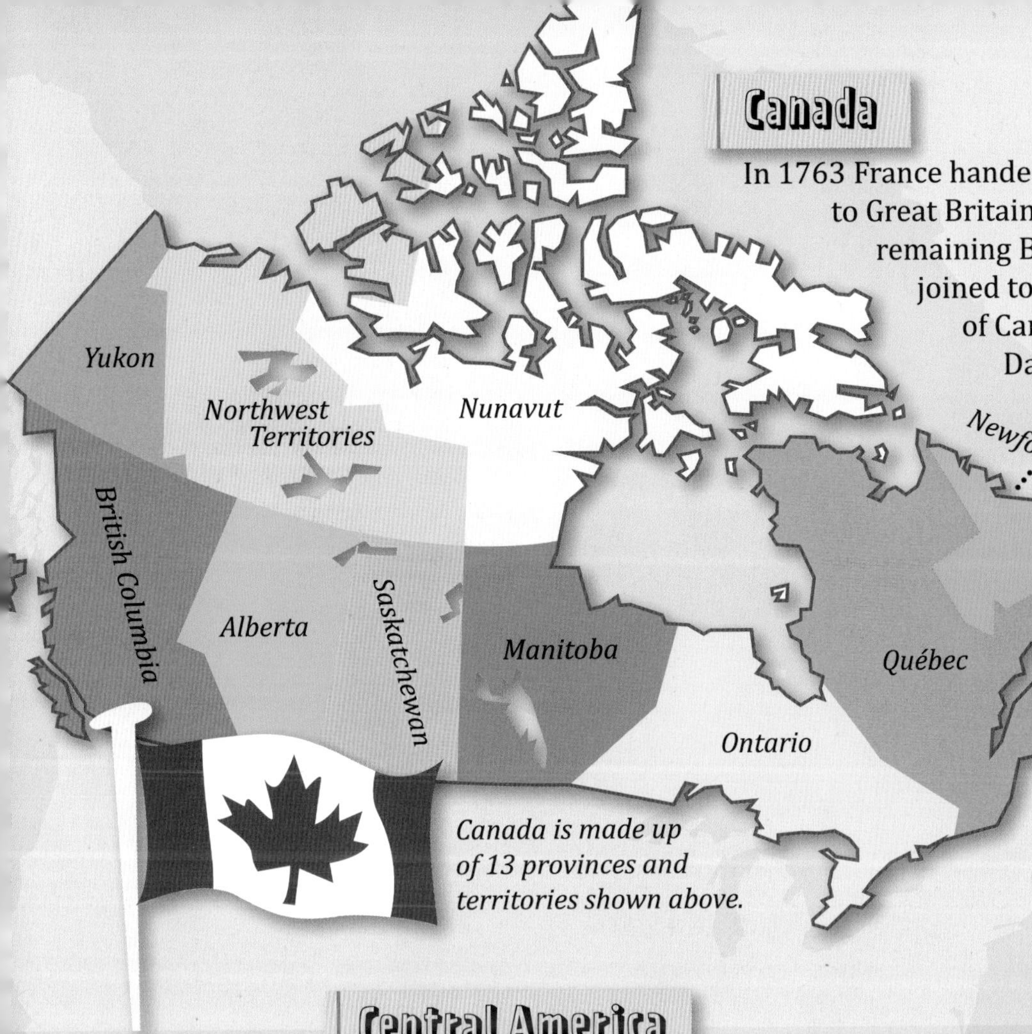

Yukon

Northwest Territories

Nunavut

British Columbia

Alberta

Saskatchewan

Manitoba

Ontario

Québec

Newfoundland and Labrador

Prince Edward Island

Nova Scotia

New Brunswick

Canada is made up of 13 provinces and territories shown above.

Central America

The Spanish colonies gained independence from Spain in 1821, forming the Mexican Empire. By 1840 the countries of Central America had declared independence, and the Mexican-American War (1846–1848) led to Mexico losing all of its territories in the modern-day USA.

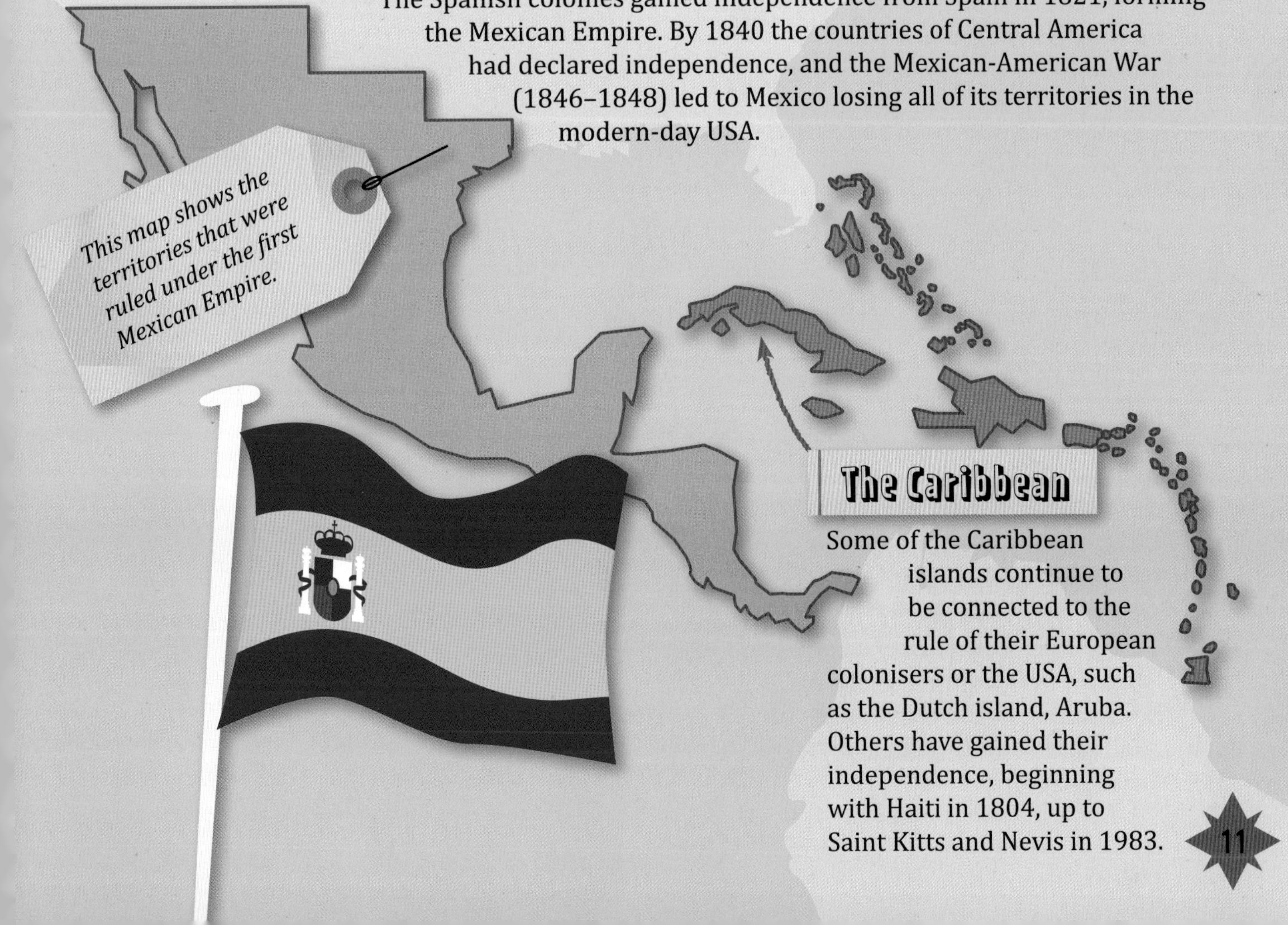

This map shows the territories that were ruled under the first Mexican Empire.

The Caribbean

Some of the Caribbean islands continue to be connected to the rule of their European colonisers or the USA, such as the Dutch island, Aruba. Others have gained their independence, beginning with Haiti in 1804, up to Saint Kitts and Nevis in 1983.

Climates

North America is positioned between two imaginary lines running horizontally across the continent in the north and south. These are the Arctic Circle and the Tropic of Cancer, areas of extreme climates, with dry to subarctic climates existing in between.

Arctic Circle

The climate within the Arctic Circle is very cold and much of the area is always covered with ice. It passes through Greenland, Canada and Alaska (USA).

Greenland

Coldest climate

Greenland has the coldest climate in North America, with 80 per cent of its mainland covered in a frozen ice sheet all year round. The average daily temperature in its capital city, Nuuk, ranges from -8°C to 7°C.

Tropic of Cancer

The Tropic of Cancer marks out a stretch of land north of the Equator. The line runs through Mexico and the Bahamas, with the area between here and the Equator known as the 'tropics'. The weather is always warm here, with the land experiencing dry and tropical climates.

Tropic of Cancer

Appalachian Mountains

Rocky Mountains

Climate zones:

- tropical
- dry
- humid subtropical
- Mediterranean
- subarctic
- polar

X = Highest average number of tornadoes a year

66
22
45 51
45
39
37
57
96
62
155
3
2
11
5

Hurricanes

Hurricanes are rotating systems of clouds and thunderstorms that form over tropical water. In North America they occur in areas that are in the Tropic of Cancer, where the water is warm. Sometimes hurricanes travel inland, causing a lot of destruction to buildings and wildlife.

Hurricane Ivan

In 2004, Hurricane Ivan travelled from the west coast of Africa towards the Caribbean and the USA. It was an incredibly destructive hurricane, causing billions of pounds' worth of damage. It was also responsible for the deaths of 121 people. As it travelled, its speed and danger level changed. A hurricane scale represents the changing stages.

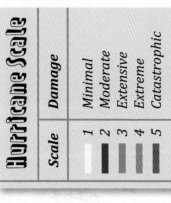

Hurricane Scale

Scale	Damage
1	Minimal
2	Moderate
3	Extensive
4	Extreme
5	Catastrophic

The hurricane season here is from June to November.

The hurricane season here is from May to October.

North American route of Hurricane Ivan

Satellite image of Hurricane Ivan off the coast of Cuba, 2004

Tornado Alley

Tornado Alley is the name given to an area that has a lot of tornado activity. In the USA this covers an area of land in the middle of America, sheltered by the Rocky Mountains and the Appalachian Mountains. In the summer, this dry climate gets very hot, with hot air from the ground rising and spinning upwards in a funnel where it meets cooler air above thunder clouds.

Wildlife

The wildlife of North America ranges from the big and furry to the small and scaly. The harsh habitats of the Arctic, the heat of the south and the changing seasons lead many creatures to migrate across the continent.

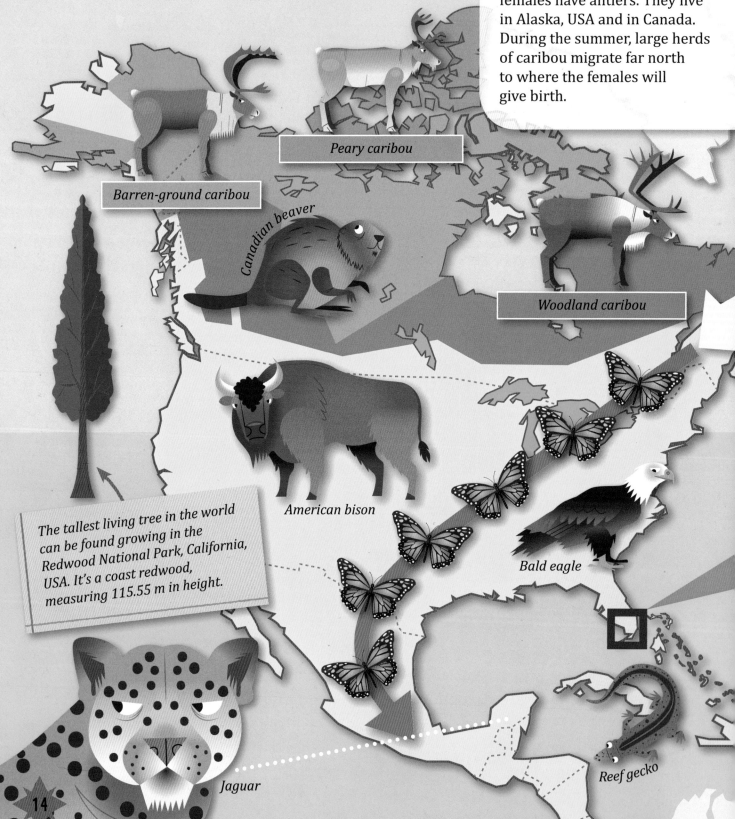

Caribou

The caribou is a member of the deer family, and is the only deer where both males and females have antlers. They live in Alaska, USA and in Canada. During the summer, large herds of caribou migrate far north to where the females will give birth.

Peary caribou

Barren-ground caribou

Canadian beaver

Woodland caribou

American bison

The tallest living tree in the world can be found growing in the Redwood National Park, California, USA. It's a coast redwood, measuring 115.55 m in height.

Bald eagle

Jaguar

Reef gecko

Monarch butterfly

Monarch butterflies migrate from the northeast of North America down to Mexico each winter, travelling up to 4,828 km. Here they hibernate in a warmer climate.

This arrow shows the migration route of the monarch butterfly.

Everglades

The Florida Everglades is one of the largest wetlands in the world. The landscape is made up of different habitats. Each habitat has many ecosystems, where a community of animals and plants interact with each other as a source of food and shelter.

Habitats of the Everglades:

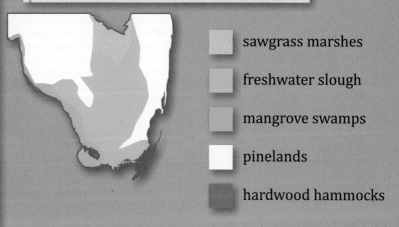

- sawgrass marshes
- freshwater slough
- mangrove swamps
- pinelands
- hardwood hammocks

The American alligator lives in the Everglades. It sits at the top of a food chain, feeding off creatures in the swamps, marshlands and the edges of the hammocks.

An Everglades food chain:

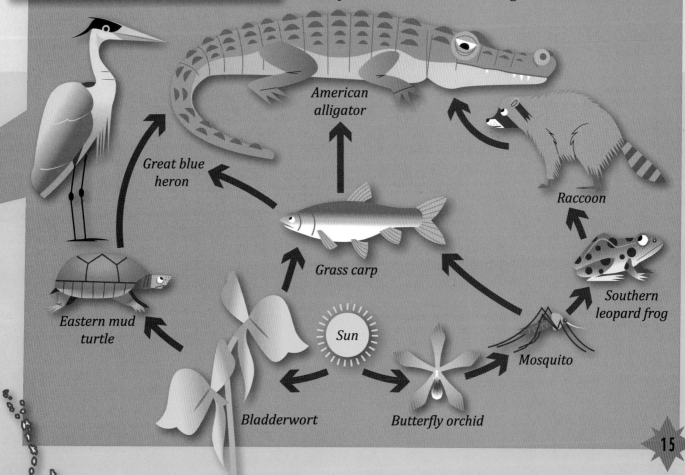

Great blue heron

American alligator

Raccoon

Grass carp

Southern leopard frog

Eastern mud turtle

Sun

Mosquito

Bladderwort

Butterfly orchid

Natural landmarks

The North American landscape ranges from vast open of plains to thick forests and dry deserts. It's also home to giant canyons, towering mountains, great lakes and awe-inspiring waterfalls.

Niagara Falls

Niagara Falls is on the border between Canada and the USA. It's made up of three waterfalls – the Horseshoe Falls, the American Falls and the Bridal Veil Falls. The Horseshoe Falls are the largest, with a vertical drop of 57 m.

The spectacular location of the Niagara Falls has encouraged many daredevils to perform dangerous feats there, such as crossing the Falls on a tightrope. In 1876, Italian Maria Spelterini managed this feat four times, once blindfolded!

Rocky Mountains

The Rocky Mountains stretch more than 4,800 km from British Columbia in Canada, down to New Mexico in the USA. Also known as the Rockies, they act as a barrier, protecting areas to the east from major winds and rains as well as from cold air travelling south from the Arctic.

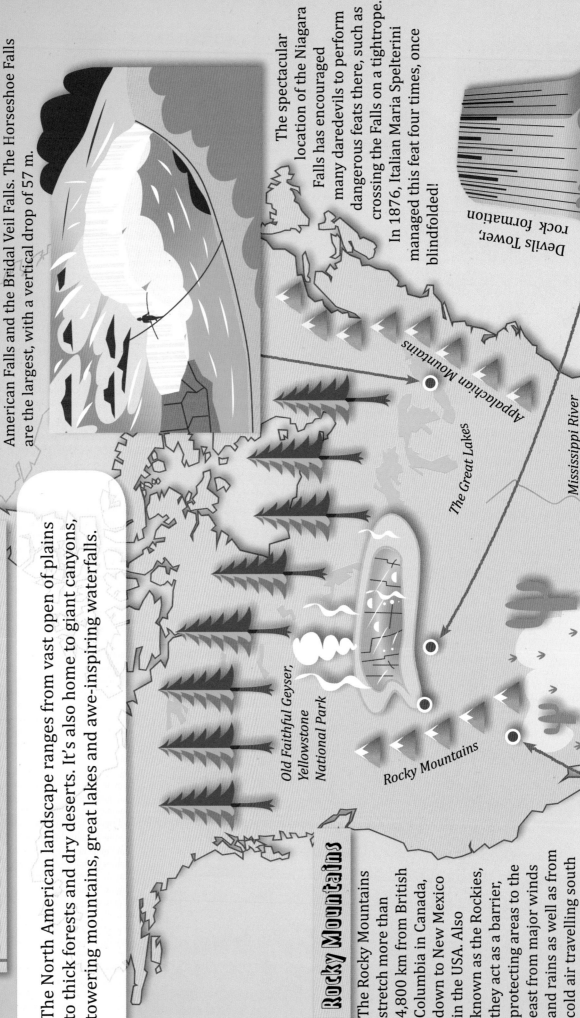

Devils Tower, rock formation

Appalachian Mountains

The Great Lakes

Mississippi River

Old Faithful Geyser, Yellowstone National Park

Rocky Mountains

Chihuahuan Desert

Great Blue Hole

An aerial view of the coast surrounding Belize reveals a deep blue circle in the ocean. This is known as the Great Blue Hole. It measures 300 m across and is 124 m deep.

It was formed from a system of limestone caves under the ocean bed that collapsed leaving a deep hole. It's believed to be the largest of its kind and is a popular site for scuba divers to explore tropical marine life.

The Grand Canyon

Around 5 million tourists visit the Grand Canyon each year. It's 433 km long, stretches 16 km across and is around 1.6 km deep. The canyon has been carved out by the Colorado River that runs through it.

Popocatépetl

Popocatépetl in Mexico is a stunning snow-capped volcano whose name means 'Smoking Mountain' in Aztec. It is one of the world's most dangerous volcanoes. A future major eruption would threaten the lives of the 20 million people who live close by in Mexico City.

Manmade landmarks

The White House, Washington D.C.

From the ancient pyramids hidden in the forests of Central America to the modern architectural feats towering in the USA, the landscape of North America is covered with manmade landmarks full of great ambition and wonder.

Mount Rushmore National Memorial

Between 1927 and 1941, the giant heads of four US presidents were sculpted into the side of Mount Rushmore in South Dakota. The monument is 18 m high, with each head the height of a six-storey building and each nose around 6 m long.

The Pentagon, Arlington County

First Nations totem pole, Vancouver Island

George Washington (1732–1799)

Theodore Roosevelt (1858–1919)

Thomas Jefferson (1743–1826)

Abraham Lincoln (1809–1865)

Disneyland castle, Florida

Golden Gate Bridge

Painted a striking orange colour, the Golden Gate Bridge opened in 1937. At the time it was the longest suspension bridge in the world. With a total length of 2,737 m, it spans the Golden Gate Strait, connecting San Francisco with Marin County.

Stone heads (Olmec)

Inukshuk, Baffin Island

Statue of Liberty

The Statue of Liberty represents the Roman goddess of freedom. It was a gift from France, presented in 1886 to celebrate American independence and the abolition of slavery. It stands at 93 m in height from the ground to the torch, welcoming boats as they pass by into New York Harbor.

Empire State Building, New York City

El Castillo

El Castillo, also known as the Temple of Kukulcán, is a step pyramid that is central to the ancient Mayan city of Chichen Itza.

The pyramid is over 1,500 years old, and was designed to reflect the Mayan calendar. There are 91 steps on each side, and with a temple platform at the top, there are a total of 365 steps, the number of days in a year.

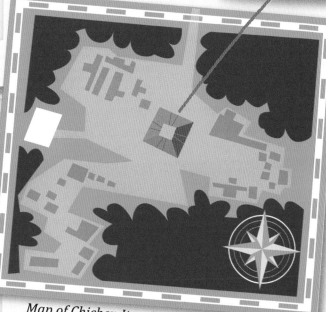

Map of Chichen Itza, in Yucatán, Mexico

Settlements

This map shows the population density of North America. The most populated areas are major cities, and the places with the least number of people are areas of vast wilderness, such as the Arctic tundra or deserts.

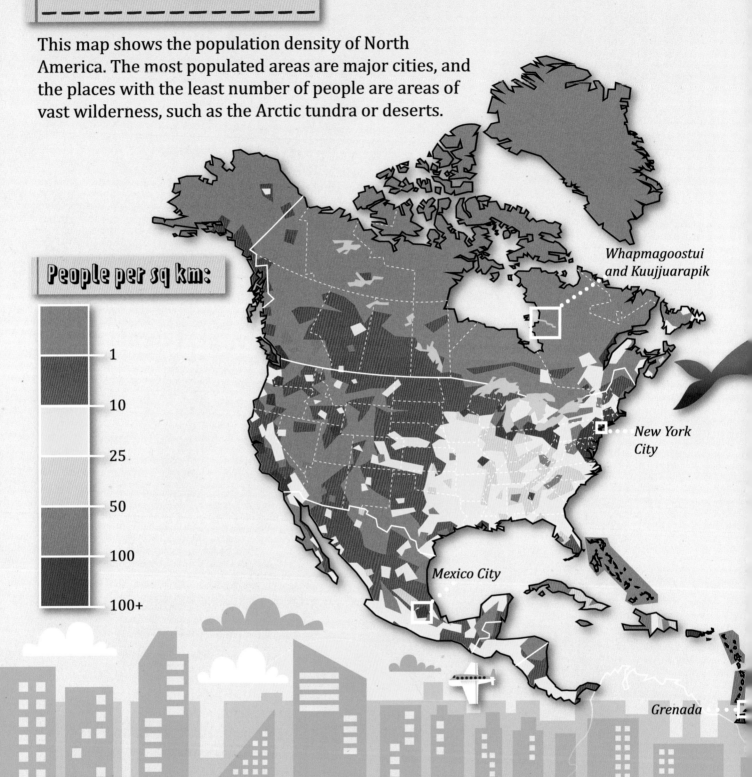

People per sq km:

1
10
25
50
100
100+

Whapmagoostui and Kuujjuarapik

New York City

Mexico City

Grenada

Mexico City

Mexico City is one of the most crowded cities in the world. It's home to 20 per cent of Mexico's population – around 9 million people. It's been estimated that the population will reach 23 million by 2020.

The city used to be swampland, where over 600 years ago the Aztecs built the city of Tenochtitlan. When the Spanish arrived in the 16th century, the Aztec city was destroyed and built over.

New York City

New York City is the most populous city in the USA. It is made up of five boroughs:

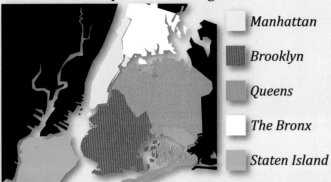

Manhattan

Brooklyn

Queens

The Bronx

Staten Island

The central streets of Manhattan were built following a simple grid layout, with blocks laid out in orderly rows. This helped safeguard against overcrowding, fire and disease, things that are harder to contain in cities with a jumbled street plan.

Whapmagoostui and Kuujjuarapik

In the northwest of Québec are two villages inhabited by two different indigenous communities.

● Kuujjuarapik

● Whapmagoostui

Great Whale River

Whapmagoostui is home to the Cree, a group of Native Americans. Less than 3 km away is Kuujjuarapik, where an Inuit community lives. Both communities settled here over 70 years ago, when it was a centre for whale hunting.

The Cree and the Inuit were traditionally nomadic people, who moved around the country building temporary homes.

The Cree used animal hides to build tipis that were easy to construct and portable.

In the winter, when out on hunts, the Inuits built temporary snowhouses, known as igloos. These were made out of blocks of tightly packed snow and could be built in around 20–30 minutes.

St George's

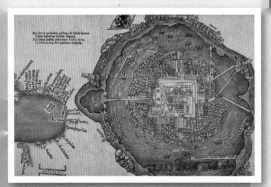

This is a map from 1524, drawn by the Spanish, showing the layout of Tenochtitlan.

The houses in the capital of Grenada, St George's, have been designed to cope with the weather and landscape.

The roofs have ridges on them, so that the rain trickles down into water tanks. • • • •

The houses are painted white to help reflect the heat of the Sun. • • • • • • • •

There is very little flat land in St George's and so the houses are built on stilts. • • • • • • • •

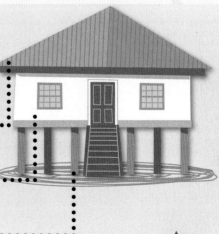

Industry

The economies of North America appear split between the north, where there are more manufacturing and hi-tech industries, and the south, where farming and tourism provide the most employment – thanks to the tropical weather and sunshine.

Main industries in North America

Crops:
- Bananas
- Corn
- Sugar cane
- Coffee
- Wheat
- Vineyards
- Tobacco

Industry:
- Car industry
- Forestry
- Hi-tech
- Textiles
- Fishing
- Tourism

Livestock:
- Cattle
- Sheep
- Pigs

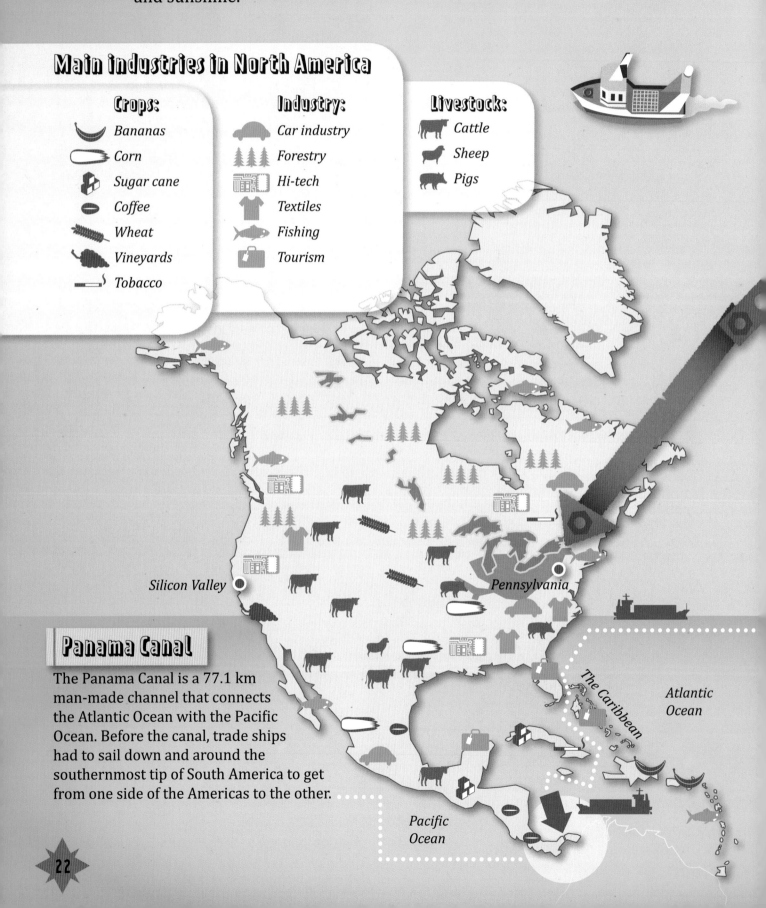

Silicon Valley

Pennsylvania

The Caribbean

Atlantic Ocean

Pacific Ocean

Panama Canal

The Panama Canal is a 77.1 km man-made channel that connects the Atlantic Ocean with the Pacific Ocean. Before the canal, trade ships had to sail down and around the southernmost tip of South America to get from one side of the Americas to the other.

Rust Belt

The northwest USA used to be called the Industrial Heartland. This area is rich with coal and iron, and housed large factories for the production of steel, cars and weapons. In the 1980s, competition from abroad led to a decline in these industries. Many people moved away to find work elsewhere and the factories were left to rust. This led the area to be known as the 'rust belt'.

An abandoned steel factory in Pennsylvania

The USA still has one of the largest manufacturing economies in the world. It leads the world in making aeroplanes and still has a strong market for US-made cars, produced by companies such as Ford and Chevrolet.

Silicon Valley

Silicon Valley is the name given to an area in California that is home to many of the world's largest technology corporations, including Apple, Facebook and Google.

The 'silicon' in its name refers to a fine sand-like material used in the making of computer chips – an essential part of products that have been made in Silicon Valley.

20,900 km

8,370 km

New York

San Francisco

Over a thousand heavily loaded ships sail through the Panama Canal each month, with the canal generating around £1.8 billion a year for Panama.

Farming

Farming is big business for all countries in North America. It's the largest industry in Central America and the Caribbean, helped by the tropical climate. Key crops include tobacco, bananas, sugar cane, coffee, cocoa beans and coconuts.

Sport

Sport is big business in North America. It's home to some of the world's top sporting legends and big sporting events, celebrating games such as baseball, basketball and American football.

Sporting profiles:

Billie Jean King

Billie Jean King is an American tennis legend. She won 39 major titles and ranked number one in the world five times between 1966 and 1972. King was a pioneer for women in sport, pushing for equal treatment and prize money.

Sporting profiles:

Usain Bolt

Nicknamed 'lightning bolt', Jamaican athlete Usain Bolt is one of the fastest sprinters in the world. In 2009 he set a new world record for the 100 m, with a time of 9.58 seconds, and in the 200 m, with a time of 19.19 seconds.

Ice hockey

While hockey has been around for hundreds of years, ice hockey has only been about since the mid-1850s. It was developed in Canada, where it is the national sport. It was originally played outdoors on iced-over ponds and rivers.

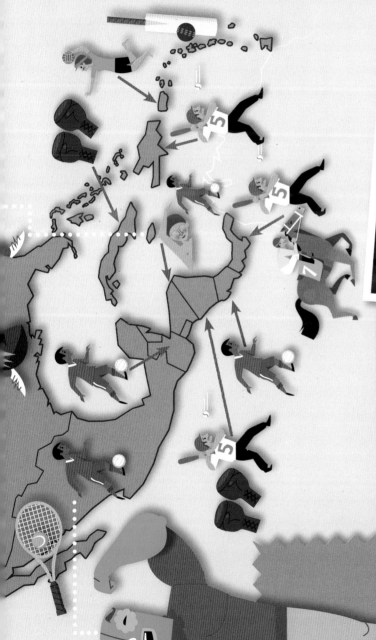

Cricket

Cricket is the most popular sport in the Caribbean. It was introduced by the British army in the early 19th century. One of the top teams in the world is the West Indies cricket team, also known as the 'Windies'. The team represents 15 Caribbean countries.

Women's football

Women's football is increasing in popularity around the world, with the USA leading the way. Their national team is one of the most successful in the world, and has won the FIFA Women's World Cup three times.

Mexican wrestling

In Mexico, professional wrestling is known as *lucha libre*. Mexican wrestling features acrobatic flying moves and the wrestlers wear colourful masks that are decorated to represent animals, gods and ancient heroes.

Culture

North America celebrates its history in festivals, storytelling and the arts. While much of its culture has a local identity, it has a reach that can be felt internationally. You only need to turn on the TV, radio or go to the cinema to see its huge influence on popular culture around the world.

Hollywood

Hollywood is a district in Los Angeles that is the centre of the US film industry. Many big film production studios have been based here since the 1920s, producing blockbuster movies that are hugely successful all around the world.

The Wild West

Mississippi River

The Wild West refers to an area of land and a time during the 19th century, when descendants of European settlers lived west of the Mississippi River. They drove across large open plains in horse-drawn wagons, with cowboys herding cattle.

There was great conflict over land between the settlers and Native American tribes who had been roaming freely. Many battles were fought, which eventually led to the destruction of the Native American way of life.

Stories of cowboys and the Wild West have since inspired many Hollywood movies.

Hip hop

Hip hop culture includes DJing, rapping, breakdancing and graffiti art. It grew out of 1970s New York, with young black Americans throwing block parties, sampling and scratching records and rapping over them. Now popular all over the world, a lot of the culture continues to be used to express feelings of race and class.

Religion

Christianity is the main religion practised throughout North America. In the Latin American countries the majority of Christians are Catholic, whereas in the USA the majority are Protestant. The colonial rulers first introduced these beliefs into the continent.

The skull is the symbol of the Day of the Dead. Some skulls are worn as masks, while others, made of chocolate and sugar, are eaten.

Day of the Dead

The Day of the Dead is a Mexican holiday where people get together to remember those that have died. Rather than being a sad occasion, it is a time of joyous celebration with parades and street parties. The dead are honoured with gifts and their gravestones are decorated with flowers.

One of the largest Roman Catholic churches in the world is the Basilica of Our Lady of Guadalupe, in Mexico City.

Food and drink

North Americans are big meat-eaters, particularly in the USA and the Caribbean. Much of the food here is influenced by European cuisine, but made with bigger portions! Maize flour forms the basis of the Central American diet, as it did in pre-Columbian times. It's used in nachos, burritos and tacos, which are now popular all over the world.

Muktuk

Muktuk is an Inuit dish of frozen whale skin and blubber. Taken from hunted narwhal, beluga or bowhead whales, the skin is rubbery and hazelnut-flavoured, while the blubber is chewy.

Fast food

Fast food is food that is prepared quickly, such as hamburgers, pizzas or fried chicken, and bought cheaply in restaurants. It first became popular in the 1950s, in the USA. The world's biggest fast-food chains, including McDonald's, KFC and Burger King, all started out in the USA.

Apple pie

Lobster

Maple syrup

Butter tart

Thanksgiving turkey

Chicago-style deep dish pizza

Creole chicken is a traditional Haitian dish. The chicken is marinated in garlic, lime and green peppers, and cooked in oil with hot red peppers, tomatoes and onion.

Creole cuisine

Creole cuisine is hot and peppery, coming from the multi-cultural heritage of French, Spanish, African and Caribbean foods and flavours. Both Haiti and Louisiana (a state in the USA) have a history of Creole culture that is reflected in their food.

Jambalaya is a popular Creole dish in Louisiana. Its ingredients include spicy sausage, peppers, onion, garlic, rice, shrimp, tomatoes, paprika and cayenne pepper.

Fried yojoa fish

Pupusa

Guacamole with tortilla chips

Tamale

The tamale dates back to the Mayan civilisation in Mexico, and is today widely eaten in all Central American countries. It's made from chopped meat and crushed peppers, packed in a parcel made from maize flour dough and wrapped in husks or leaves, then steamed.

Further information

COUNTRY	SIZE SQ KM	POPULATION	CAPITAL CITY	MAIN LANGUAGES
USA	9,826,675	321,368,864	Washington, D.C.	English
Mexico	1,964,375	121,736,809	Mexico City	Spanish
Canada	9,984,670	35,099,836	Ottawa	English, French
Guatemala	108,889	14,918,999	Guatemala City	Spanish
Cuba	110,860	11,031,433	Havana	Spanish
Dominican Republic	48,670	10,478,756	Santo Domingo	Spanish
Haiti	27,750	10,110,019	Port-au-Prince	French, Haitian Creole
Honduras	112,090	8,746,673	Tegucigalp	Spanish
El Salvador	21,041	6,125,512	San Salvador	Spanish
Nicaragua	130,370	5,907,881	Managua	Spanish
Costa Rica	51,100	4,814,144	San José	Spanish
Panama	75,420	3,657,024	Panama City	Spanish
Jamaica	10,991	2,950,210	Kingston	English
Trinidad and Tobago	5,128	1,222,363	Port of Spain	English
Belize	22,966	347,369	Belmopan	English, Spanish
Bahamas	13,880	324,597	Nassau	English
Barbados	430	290,604	Bridgetown	English
Saint Lucia	616	163,922	Castries	English
Grenada	344	110,694	St George's	Dutch, Papiamento
Saint Vincent and the Grenadines	389	102,627	Kingstown	English
Antigua and Barbuda	442.6	92,436	St John's	English
Dominica	751	73,607	Roseau	English
Greenland	2,166,086	57,733	Nuuk	Greenlandic, Danish
Saint Kitts and Nevis	261	51,936	Basseterre	English

Glossary

blubber
a layer of fat found between the skin and muscle of a whale

climate
average weather conditions in a particular area

colonial
relating to the colonies – countries or areas controlled by another country and occupied by settlers from that country

dry
a climate zone that receives little rainfall with land that can be too dry to support much vegetation; experienced in areas such as deserts and grasslands

empire
a group of countries governed under a single authority, such as under one ruler or country

Equator
an imaginary line drawn around the Earth separating the Northern and Southern hemispheres

fjord
a long narrow inlet of water between steep walls of rock

food chain
a series of organisms; each is dependent on the next organism lower down the chain as a source of food

glacier
a mass of ice that moves slowly over a large area of land

hammocks
an elevated area of fertile land, usually with hardwood trees and surrounded by wetlands

heritage
items of historical importance for a country, such as buildings, as well as traditions from the past

humid subtropical
a climate zone characterised by hot, humid summers and mild to cool winters

immigrants
people who come to live permanently in a foreign country

indigenous peoples
communities living in a particular country or region that have lived there long before the invasion and settlement of a foreign society, such as the Native Americans in the USA

Mediterranean
a climate zone with long, hot and dry summers and cool, wet winters

migration
seasonal movement of animals from one region to another

pioneer
the first person to do something; someone who leads the way in exploring something new

polar
climate zones found surrounding the North and South Poles, which are extremely cold and dry

slough
an area of marshy river with slow-moving water

subarctic
a climate zone that is found in areas south of the Arctic Circle, experiencing long, cold winters and short, cool to mild summers

supercontinent
a former large continent made up of several present-day continents that broke off and drifted away

tropical
a climate zone with hot and humid weather and high temperatures throughout the year

wetland
an area of land covered in shallow water, such as a swamp or marsh

Index